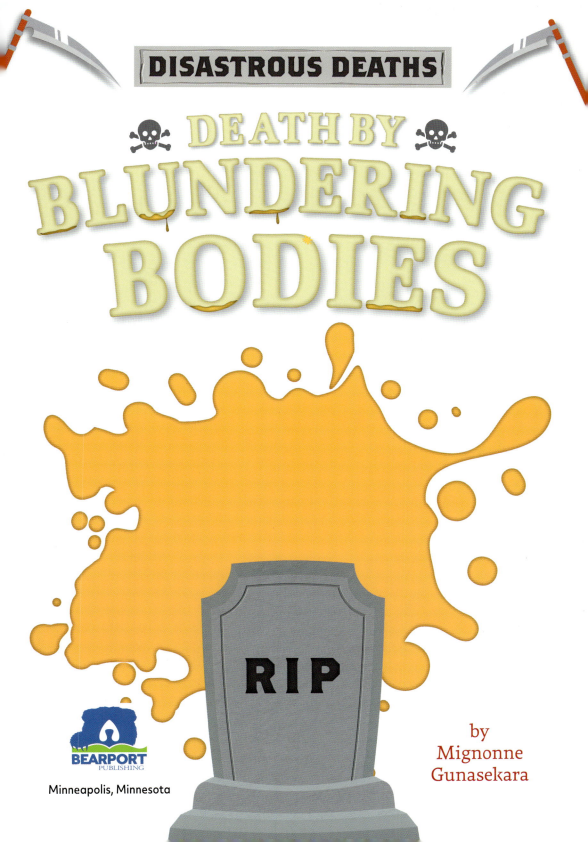

DISASTROUS DEATHS

DEATH BY BLUNDERING BODIES

BEARPORT PUBLISHING
Minneapolis, Minnesota

by Mignonne Gunasekara

Library of Congress Cataloging-in-Publication Data

Names: Gunasekara, Mignonne, author.
Title: Death by blundering bodies / by Mignonne Gunasekara.
Description: Minneapolis, MN : Bearport Publishing, [2022] | Series: Disastrous deaths | Includes bibliographical references and index.
Identifiers: LCCN 2020058667 (print) | LCCN 2020058668 (ebook) | ISBN 9781636911656 (library binding) | ISBN 9781636911700 (ebook)
Subjects: LCSH: Biography–Miscellanea–Juvenile literature. | Death–Miscellanea–Juvenile literature.
Classification: LCC CT105 .G86 2022 (print) | LCC CT105 (ebook) | DDC 920–dc23
LC record available at https://lccn.loc.gov/2020058667
LC ebook record available at https://lccn.loc.gov/2020058668

© 2022 Booklife Publishing
This edition is published by arrangement with Booklife Publishing.

North American adaptations © 2022 Bearport Publishing Company. All rights reserved. No part of this publication may be reproduced in whole or in part, stored in any retrieval system, or transmitted in any form or by any means, electronic, mechanical, photocopying, recording, or otherwise, without written permission from the publisher.

For more information, write to Bearport Publishing, 5357 Penn Avenue South, Minneapolis, MN 55419. Printed in the United States of America.

PHOTO CREDITS

All images are courtesy of Shutterstock.com, unless otherwise specified. With thanks to Getty Images, Thinkstock Photo, and iStockphoto. Background texture throughout - Abstracto. Gravestone throughout - MaryValery. Front Cover - Panda Vector, Taleseedum. 5 - Graphic Treasure, Praisaeng. 7 - Marko Poplasen. 8 - Giuseppe Porta [Public domain], Tim UR. 9 - British Museum [Public domain], romawka, ONYXprj. 11 - ONYXprj, Valentin Agapov. 12 - https://commons.wikimedia.org/wiki/File:Hans_Staininger.jpg, Mathew Brady [Public domain], Paper Teo, Christophe BOISSON, Migren Art, Alfmaler, PegasuStudio. 13 - Olga Popova, Roger Higgins, World Telegram staff photographer [Public domain], ONYXprj, . 14 - Antonov Maxim, Uncimo. 15 - guteksk7. 16 - Frederico Moeller, Eduard Ender (1822-1883) [Public domain], StockVector. 17 - SvetlanaSF, lynea, Colorcocktail, mStudioVector. 18 - ONYXprj. 19 - bioraven, Nora Hachio. 20 - Everett Historical, Hong Vo, ONYXprj, Oceloti, ImLucky. 21 - Alan Kelly, oranoot, KittyVector, Anna.zabella. 22 - Macrovector. 23 - NataliaVo. 24 - Mick Atkins, VectorArtFactory. 25 - gabriel12. 27 - artbesouro, Mountain Brothers. 28 - unknown, after Francis Cotes (1726-1770) [Public domain], Super8, Waeel quttene, SilviaC. 29 - donsimon, National Portrait Gallery [Public domain]*, Elegant Solution, Vector Plotnikoff, Morphart Creation. * - U.S. work public domain in the U.S. for unspecified reason but presumably because it was published in the U.S. before 1924.
Additional illustrations by Jasmine Pointer.

CONTENTS

Welcome to the Disaster Zone 4

Chrysippus of Soli 6

What's So Funny? 8

Hans Steininger 10

Hairy Business 12

Tycho Brahe 14

Mind Your Manners 16

Sir Francis Bacon 18

Snow Way to Go 20

Frank Hayes 22

You Win Some, You Lose Some . . 24

Maria Gunning 26

Beauty Is Pain 28

Timeline of Deaths 30

Glossary 31

Index 32

Read More 32

WELCOME TO THE DISASTER ZONE

As any history book will tell you, people have led some pretty wild and crazy lives. So it's no surprise that their deaths have been pretty weird and wacky, too. From holding their pee too long and laughing themselves senseless, to tripping over their own beards and poisoning themselves with makeup, people have found some pretty creative ways to blunder into the great beyond.

Since the beginning of human history, about 107 billion people have lived on Earth. You know what that means . . . there are lots of deaths to choose from!

In this book, we are going to look at the stories of six people who were taken out by their own blundering bodies and discover the many bizarre ways in which these and other unlucky people met their disastrous ends.

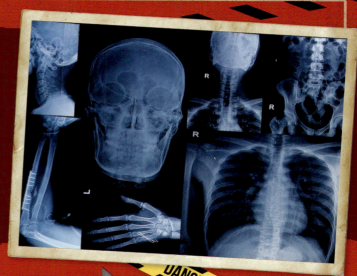

INTO THE DISASTER ZONE WE GO . . .

Throughout history, there have been lots of sayings that mean someone has died.

Here are a few of the weird ones:

- Kicked the bucket
- Bit the dust
- Met their maker
- Six feet under
- Food for worms
- Pushing up daisies

CHRYSIPPUS OF SOLI

Chrysippus was an ancient Greek **philosopher**. He was born in Soli, an area that is now part of Turkey, but later he moved to Athens. There, he became head of a school of philosophy.

One day, Chrysippus saw a donkey eating figs and joked that someone should give the donkey some wine to wash them down. He thought this was all so funny that he laughed himself to death. I guess you had to be there. . . .

Philosophy involves asking questions about how people should live their lives.

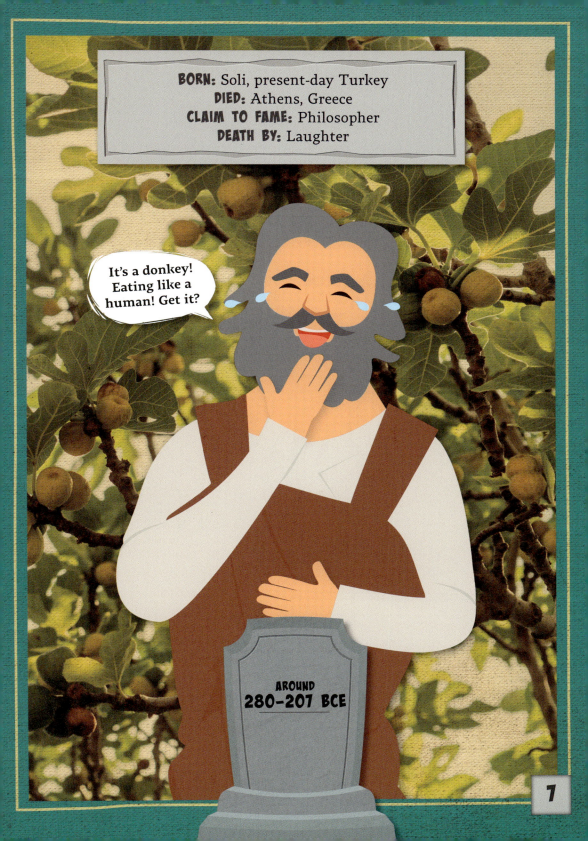

WHAT'S SO FUNNY?

Despite Chrysippus's fatal case of the giggles, he was considered a Stoic philosopher. This philosophy says self-control and strength are important in order to be calm and avoid showing emotion. They believed if you are calm, you can make better choices.

A drawing of Chrysippus laughing at the donkey

Chrysippus must have found that donkey really funny if he lost his Stoic control and laughed himself to death.

Stoics believed the way to make good choices and live a good life was to use **logic**.

Figs

8

Chrysippus's Contribution

Chrysippus wrote more than 700 works about Stoicism. Sadly, none of them survived.

Hey, a donkey's gotta eat.

Chrysippus

Chrysippus wrote at least 500 lines each day. He loved **debating** and looking at both sides of an argument.

In his writing, Chrysippus even argued both sides of an idea.

HANS STEININGER

Hans Steininger was the mayor of Braunau am Inn, Austria, during the sixteenth century. He was famous for his incredibly long beard, which was around 4.5 feet (1.4 m) long! To keep it out of the way, Hans would stuff his beard into a pouch or pocket. In 1567, a large fire raced through town. Hans died when he tripped over his beard on his way down some stairs. He hadn't been able to tuck his beard out of the way before running from the fire.

Hans's beard was put on display in Braunau's District Museum. You can still go to see it today.

BORN: Pfarrkirchen, Germany
DIED: Braunau am Inn, Austria
CLAIM TO FAME: His long beard
DEATH BY: His long beard

Why didn't I trim this thing?!

DIED 1567

HAIRY BUSINESS

Hans isn't the only person in history with famous facial hair. Let's take a look at a few others.

Ambrose Burnside

Ambrose Burnside was a general during the Civil War (1861–1865). His wondrous whiskers set the trend for this now-famous style of facial hair, which was eventually named sideburns.

Hans Steininger

Ambrose Burnside

Hair grows about half an inch (1.25 cm) a month—the only other part of the body that grows faster is **bone marrow**.

Edward Teach

Edward Teach is better known by another name —Blackbeard. This famous eighteenth-century pirate wore his beard in **dreadlocks**, with slow-burning **fuses** wound into them. Before any sea battle, Edward would light the fuses so that smoke **billowed** from his beard. This (rightly) terrified his opponent!

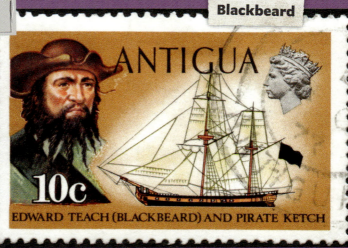
Blackbeard

Salvador Dalí

Salvador Dalí was a Spanish artist who made very strange paintings. But the strangest thing about him may have been his mustache.

Salvador Dalí's body was dug up in 2017, and his mustache was still perfectly styled!

Salvador Dalí

TYCHO BRAHE

Tycho Brahe was a sixteenth-century Danish **astronomer**. Over the years, he made notes on more than 1,000 new stars! There is even a crater on the moon named after him.

One night at a banquet, Tycho realized he needed to pee. In those days, however, people thought that getting up in the middle of a meal was rude. So, polite Tycho held his pee and kept eating and drinking. Tycho became very sick and died just 11 days later.

Some people thought that Tycho was actually poisoned to death with **mercury**, but experts now think he hurt his organs by holding in his pee.

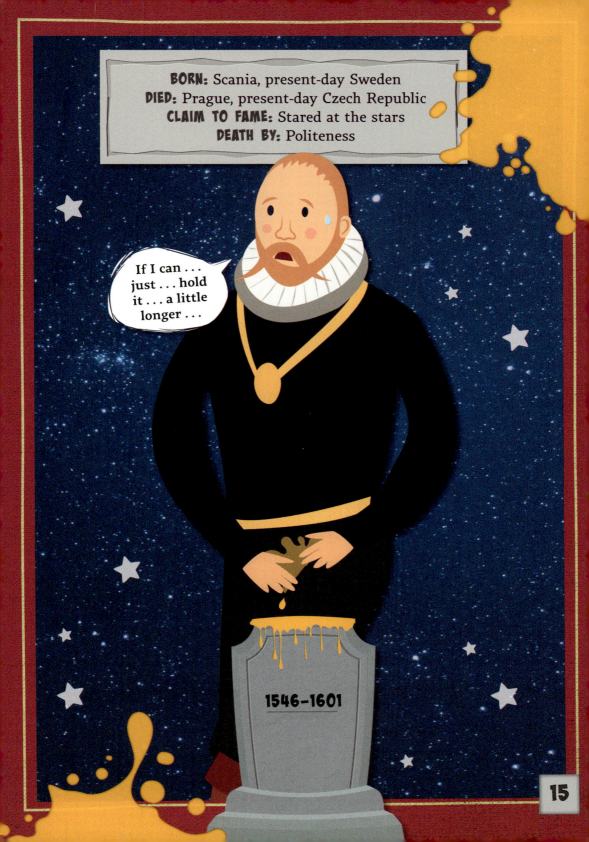

MIND YOUR MANNERS

Murder Most Foul?

Who would have wanted Tycho out of the way enough to poison him? Some scientists thought that astronomer Johannes Kepler could have wanted to poison Tycho. At the time, he lived with Tycho as an assistant, so Johannes definitely had the chance to poison him.

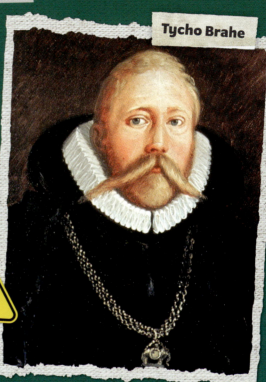

Tycho Brahe

This is the crater named after Tycho.

In 1566, Tycho lost part of his nose in a sword fight and had to wear a metal **prosthetic** for the rest of his life.

Funny about Forks

Good table manners have changed over the years. There was a time when people used only knives to eat. They also wiped their hands on the tablecloth instead of napkins!

A table fit for a banquet

In 1533, Catherine de Medici married the future king of France, Henry II. Catherine had grown up in Italy and was used to eating with a fork. People in France laughed at her because they did not use forks to eat.

Catherine de Medici

People may not have liked forks because they looked like pitchforks, which they associated with the devil.

SIR FRANCIS BACON

The early seventeenth-century **statesman**, philosopher, and scientist Sir Francis Bacon was a man of many talents and creative solutions to problems.

A bright idea came to him on a cold winter's day when he was taking a carriage ride through London. Sir Francis wondered if snow could keep uncooked meat fresh. He stopped the carriage, bought an uncooked chicken, and stuffed it full of snow to see if his idea was correct. Handling the cold snow apparently made Sir Francis very sick, and he died soon afterwards.

Some say the ghost of the chicken that Sir Francis stuffed with snow still roams around Highgate, squawking and flapping its wings.

BORN: London, England
DIED: London, England
CLAIM TO FAME: Being really clever
DEATH BY: Frozen chicken

I can't feel my hands!

1561–1626

SNOW WAY TO GO

Sir Francis was definitely onto something—low temperatures do keep foods fresher for longer. So how did people keep their food from spoiling before fridges and freezers were available?

Sir Francis Bacon

Keepin' It Fresh

It is thought that ancient cultures used wind and the warm sunlight to dry and preserve their food.

Beef jerky is made by drying pieces of beef. It doesn't need to be kept in the fridge.

20

Frozen fish

People who lived in cold parts of the world froze their meat by burying it in the snow or underground.

Brr-illiant Birdseye

Clarence Birdseye caused a stir in the frozen food industry with his method of quick freezing. Clarence was inspired by the Inuit people of Canada who froze fish as soon as they were caught. The fish still tasted fresh when it was cooked much later.

The door to an old ice cellar

People used ice cellars or ice houses to store ice and chill or freeze food.

FRANK HAYES

In the summer of 1923, Frank Hayes won first place in a horse race at Belmont Park in New York. He rode a horse called Sweet Kiss, and together they crossed the finish line far ahead of all the other racers. But when people gathered around Frank to congratulate him after the race, they got a freaky surprise. Frank was dead!

Frank had died from a heart attack during the race but somehow didn't fall out of the saddle. That's determination!

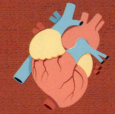

After this deadly race, Sweet Kiss became known as Sweet Kiss of Death.

YOU WIN SOME, YOU LOSE SOME

Horse races can be very eventful. Let's take a look at other interesting racing stories.

Equine Imposter

In 1844, the winner of the Epsom Derby was **disqualified** for cheating. The oldest a horse was allowed to be to compete in the race was three years old, but the winner was actually four years old. The horse's owner had dyed its hair to make it look younger!

Even being just one year older makes a horse bigger, stronger, and more likely to win a race.

Never Mind, Take Two

A steeplechase in 1945 had a record set . . . for the slowest winning time ever! A horse named Never Mind II refused to jump over a fence, so his rider gave up and left the racetrack.

A racehorse and jockey jumping over a **hurdle** during a steeplechase race

Never Mind II's rider then heard that all the other horses in the race had been disqualified or had not finished. So the two of them returned to the track and ended up winning with a time of 11 minutes and 28 seconds.

A steeplechase is a race where horses have to leap over hurdles.

MARIA GUNNING

Maria Gunning was an eighteenth-century actress in London. She had countless fans waiting for her by the stage door after every performance. Maria's life was going well, but something was eating away at her—quite literally.

The makeup she wore everyday contained mercury and **lead**, substances which we now know are poisonous. They caused the skin to melt off Maria's face. This only made her apply more of the **toxic** makeup to try to cover up the scars. Maria eventually died of makeup poisoning!

Maria's fans were so obsessed with her that she needed bodyguards to keep her safe when she went for walks.

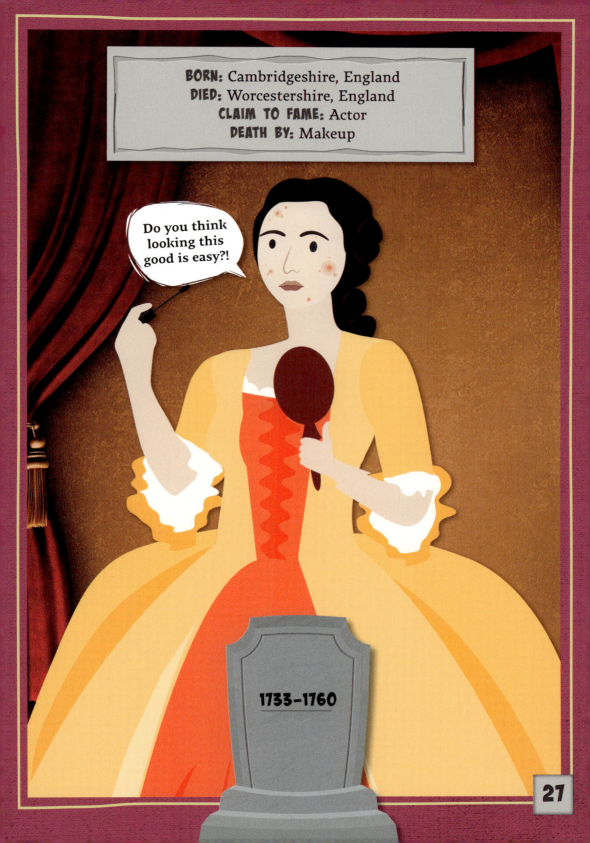

BEAUTY IS PAIN

In Maria Gunning's day, white skin and rosy cheeks were thought to be very beautiful. If you wanted to make your skin whiter and your cheeks rosier, there were products you could buy to help... but the cost was deadly!

Maria used a product made with lead to whiten her skin. The powder she used on her cheeks and her red lipstick both contained mercury. In these amounts, lead and mercury are deadly.

Maria Gunning

An ancient eyeliner pot

An antique powder box

Lead and mercury in the makeup seeped into Maria's skin and then into her blood.

Maybe She's Born with It, Maybe It's Lead Poisoning

Ancient Greek and Roman women also used to whiten their faces with lead-based makeup. Ancient Egyptians wore eyeliner with lead as protection from sunlight and illness.

Makeup can be found all over the world and throughout history.

Lead would make a person's skin change color, make their hair fall out, and make their teeth crumble. This is said to have happened to Queen Elizabeth I of England.

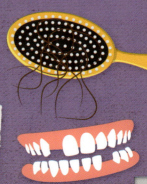

Queen Elizabeth I wanted to cover up her smallpox scars with makeup.

TIMELINE OF DEATHS

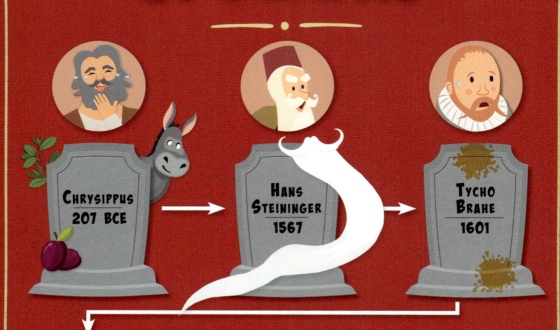
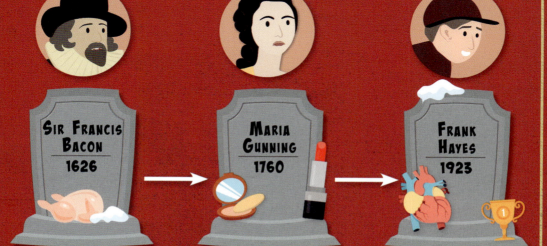

GLOSSARY

astronomer a person who studies objects in space

billowed spread out like a puffy wave

bone marrow spongy tissue found inside some bones in the body, including the hip and thigh bones

debating having a formal or serious discussion about a topic

disqualified not counted because of something done that was against the rules

dreadlocks a hairstyle that involves twisting sections of hair into thick strands

fuses pieces of rope or other materials that have been soaked in something that can be lit on fire

hurdle one of a series of barriers to jump over in a race

lead a heavy, soft, gray metal that is poisonous if eaten or absorbed into a person's body

logic a clear and reasonable way to use careful thought to make decisions

mercury a silver liquid-like metal that is poisonous if eaten or absorbed into a person's body

philosopher a person who studies the nature of knowledge, reality, and life

posthumous happening after death

prosthetic a human-made body part that is often used to replace a natural one that has been lost or damaged

statesman a wise, skilled, and respected government leader or representative

toxic poisonous

INDEX

ancient cultures 20
beards 4, 10–11, 13
debating 9
donkeys 6–9
fires 10
food 5, 20–21
forks 17
Greece 6–7, 29
horses 22–25
Kepler, Johannes 16
laughter 4, 6–8, 17

lead 26, 28–29
makeup 4, 26–29
manners 16–17
mercury 14, 26, 28
mustaches 13
pee 4, 14
philosophy 6, 8
pirates 13
poison 4, 14, 16, 26
racing 22–25
snow 18, 21

READ MORE

Croy, Anita. *Terrible and Toxic Makeup (The Bizarre History of Beauty)*. New York: Gareth Stevens Publishing, 2019.

Finan, Catherine C. *Ancient Greece (X-treme Facts: Ancient History)*. Minneapolis: Bearport Publishing, 2022.

Garrison, Hal. *Barrel Racing (Daredevil Sports)*. New York: Gareth Stevens Publishing, 2018.